SOLVING EQUATIONS USING THE ORDER OF OPERATIONS

Math Workbooks Grade 6
Children's Math Books

Speedy Publishing LLC

40 E. Main St. #1156

Newark, DE 19711

www.speedypublishing.com

Copyright 2017

Order of Operations (BEDMAS)

In mathematics, we use brackets to group parts of an expression into sub-expressions. We commonly use parentheses (), but we may also use square brackets [ ], or curly brackets {}.

BEDMAS tells us to evaluate what's in the brackets first. But what is BEDMAS?

BEDMAS is an acronym that reminds us of the correct order of operations:

Brackets	**First Priority**
Exponents	**Second Priority**
Division	**Third Priority**
Multiplication	**Third Priority**
Addition	**Fourth Priority**
Subtraction	**Fourth Priority**

BEDMAS tells us that brackets are the highest priority, then exponents, then both division and multiplication, and finally addition and subtraction. This means that we evaluate exponents before we multiply, divide before we subtract, etc.

INSTRUCTIONS

RULE 1: First perform any calculations inside the parentheses.

RULE 2: Next perform all multiplications and divisions, working from left to right.

RULE 3: Lastly, perform all additions and subtractions, working from left to right.

Example

Evaluate 3 + 6 x (5 + 4) ÷ 3 - 7 using the order of operations.

Solution:

Step 1:	3 + 6 x (5 + 4) ÷ 3 - 7 =	3 + 6 x 9 ÷ 3 - 7	Parentheses
Step 2:	3 + 6 x 9 ÷ 3 - 7 =	3 + 54 ÷ 3 - 7	Multiplication
Step 3:	3 + 54 ÷ 3 - 7 =	3 + 18 - 7	Division
Step 4:	3 + 18 - 7 =	21 - 7	Addition
Step 5:	21 - 7 =	14	Subtraction

EXERCISE NO. 1

Use the right order of operations to find the answer.

(1) $6 \times 27 \div 9 =$

(2) $5 \times 10 \times 4 =$

(3) $4 + 6 + 6 =$

(4) $42 \div 7 \times 7 =$

(5) $9 \times 9 \times 3 =$

(6) $9 + 8 + 35 - 7 =$

(7) $12 - 6 + 12 - 6 =$

(8) $4 + 3 + 6 + 5 =$

(9) $15 - 3 + 10 + 7 =$

(10) $9 \times 32 \div 8 =$

EXERCISE NO. 2

Use the right order of operations to find the answer.

(1) $40 \div 10 \times 2 =$

(2) $15 \div 5 + 3 =$

(3) $8 + 6 \times 21 - 7 =$

(4) $5 \times 7 + 4 =$

(5) $9 \times 10 + 6 =$

(6) $3 + 4 + 4 =$

(7) $10 - 5 + 70 \div 10 =$

(8) $10 \times 5 + 7 =$

(9) $6 \times 4 \times 6 =$

(10) $3 \times 8 \div 4 + 7 =$

EXERCISE NO. 3

Use the right order of operations to find the answer.

(1) $36 \div 6 \times 3 =$

(2) $7 + 9 \times 2 =$

(3) $6 \times 10 + 56 \div 7 =$

(4) $6 + 15 \div 5 =$

(5) $4 \times 8 \times 8 \div 4 =$

(6) $6 + 6 + 7 \times 9 =$

(7) $80 \div 10 \times 7 =$

(8) $25 - 5 + 42 \div 6 =$

(9) $3 + 50 \div 5 =$

(10) $9 + 2 + 3 =$

EXERCISE NO. 4

Use the right order of operations to find the answer.

(1) $2 + 6 + 2 \times 9 =$

(2) $10 \div 5 + 8 =$

(3) $5 \times 2 + 3 =$

(4) $8 \times 10 + 18 - 9 =$

(5) $3 \times 54 \div 9 =$

(6) $8 \times 5 + 5 =$

(7) $8 - 2 + 3 =$

(8) $6 \times 5 + 6 =$

(9) $2 \times 16 - 4 =$

(10) $7 + 6 \times 9 \times 6 =$

EXERCISE NO. 5

Use the right order of operations to find the answer.

(1) $5 \times 25 - 5 =$

(2) $48 \div 8 + 7 =$

(3) $5 \times 42 \div 7 =$

(4) $4 + 70 \div 10 \times 2 =$

(5) $5 \times 14 - 48 \div 8 =$

(6) $6 + 5 + 48 \div 6 =$

(7) $20 \div 2 + 2 =$

(8) $8 + 16 - 4 =$

(9) $3 + 9 + 4 =$

(10) $5 \times 30 - 10 \times 9 =$

EXERCISE NO. 6

Use the right order of operations to find the answer.

(1) $6 + 10 + 50 \div 10 =$

(2) $4 + 12 - 4 =$

(3) $2 + 8 + 32 \div 8 =$

(4) $9 - 14 \div 2 =$

(5) $2 \times 27 - 9 =$

(6) $10 \times 6 - 2 =$

(7) $24 \div 8 + 8 =$

(8) $3 \times 35 - 32 - 8 =$

(9) $20 - 9 - 3 =$

(10) $8 \times 20 - 5 \times 3 =$

EXERCISE NO. 7

Use the right order of operations to find the answer.

(1) $10 \times 20 - 4 =$

(2) $40 - 8 + 7 + 9 =$

(3) $6 + 3 + 8 + 10 =$

(4) $2 + 5 \times 8 \times 6 =$

(5) $5 + 10 - 2 =$

(6) $8 - 4 + 2 \times 7 =$

(7) $2 + 54 \div 6 =$

(8) $2 \times 8 \times 8 =$

(9) $2 \times 12 \div 4 =$

(10) $9 \times 12 \div 2 + 6 =$

EXERCISE NO. 8

Use the right order of operations to find the answer.

(1) $40 - 15 - 5 =$

(2) $3 \times 64 \div 8 =$

(3) $6 \times 9 \div 3 + 7 =$

(4) $2 + 8 \times 4 \times 7 =$

(5) $5 + 8 + 6 \times 10 =$

(6) $5 + 10 \times 8 + 2 =$

(7) $10 \times 7 + 2 =$

(8) $7 \times 12 - 6 =$

(9) $9 + 9 - 3 =$

(10) $8 + 3 \times 3 =$

EXERCISE NO. 9

Use the right order of operations to find the answer.

(1) $2 + 5 \times 9 =$

(2) $8 \times 8 + 4 \times 10 =$

(3) $12 - 4 + 2 =$

(4) $25 \div 5 + 3 =$

(5) $8 + 4 + 24 - 8 =$

(6) $70 \div 7 \times 7 =$

(7) $8 - 2 + 2 + 2 =$

(8) $5 \times 14 - 7 =$

(9) $3 + 12 - 6 =$

(10) $7 + 8 + 20 - 5 =$

EXERCISE NO. 10

Use the right order of operations to find the answer.

(1) $10 - 2 + 2 =$

(2) $7 \times 10 - 2 =$

(3) $72 \div 9 + 16 \div 2 =$

(4) $14 \div 7 \times 12 \div 3 =$

(5) $8 + 6 + 28 \div 7 =$

(6) $4 \times 20 - 8 - 2 =$

(7) $21 \div 7 \times 6 =$

(8) $15 \div 5 \times 6 \times 3 =$

(9) $24 \div 3 + 5 =$

(10) $5 + 6 \times 3 =$

EXERCISE NO. 11

Use the right order of operations to find the answer.

(1) $32 \div 8 \times 9 + 8 =$

(2) $7 + 10 + 7 =$

(3) $2 + 35 \div 5 + 6 =$

(4) $8 + 30 - 27 \div 9 =$

(5) $50 - 10 \div 2 =$

(6) $30 - 10 + 3 =$

(7) $4 - 2 + 6 =$

(8) $10 \times 2 \times 7 =$

(9) $6 + 40 \div 10 =$

(10) $9 \times 24 \div 8 + 9 =$

EXERCISE NO. 12

Use the right order of operations to find the answer.

(1) $36 \div 12 \div 3 + 3 =$

(2) $3 + 35 - 7 =$

(3) $27 \div 3 + 6 \times 5 =$

(4) $2 + 5 \times 4 + 5 =$

(5) $9 \times 40 \div 5 =$

(6) $8 \times 3 + 7 =$

(7) $9 \times 49 \div 7 =$

(8) $3 \times 28 - 21 \div 7 =$

(9) $8 + 28 - 16 - 8 =$

(10) $20 \div 2 + 8 =$

EXERCISE NO. 13

Use the right order of operations to find the answer.

(1) $16 \div 8 + 30 - 6 =$

(2) $4 + 3 + 9 =$

(3) $14 \div 2 + 6 =$

(4) $8 \times 14 - 7 =$

(5) $9 + 6 + 6 - 2 =$

(6) $6 + 24 \div 8 - 4 =$

(7) $7 + 7 + 7 =$

(8) $30 \div 6 + 24 \div 4 =$

(9) $21 - 6 - 2 \times 4 =$

(10) $18 \div 9 \times 7 =$

EXERCISE NO. 14

Use the right order of operations to find the answer.

(1) $18 \div 2 + 8 + 8 =$

(2) $8 \times 6 + 4 =$

(3) $7 + 25 - 5 =$

(4) $36 - 48 \div 12 \div 2 =$

(5) $10 \times 10 \div 2 + 8 =$

(6) $4 \times 3 + 8 =$

(7) $32 - 15 \div 5 + 7 =$

(8) $30 \div 5 + 8 + 10 =$

(9) $5 \times 10 \times 10 =$

(10) $9 \times 3 \times 6 =$

EXERCISE NO. 15

Use the right order of operations to find the answer.

(1) $9 + 2 + 9 =$

(2) $7 + 20 - 4 =$

(3) $10 \times 3 + 18 - 9 =$

(4) $32 - 9 - 3 =$

(5) $63 \div 7 \times 6 \div 2 =$

(6) $8 \times 3 + 3 =$

(7) $15 - 5 + 2 + 8 =$

(8) $60 \div 4 - 2 =$

(9) $18 - 10 - 2 =$

(10) $4 \times 4 + 2 =$

EXERCISE NO. 16

Use the right order of operations to find the answer.

(1) $30 - 6 \times 3 + 4 =$

(2) $6 \times 90 \div 9 =$

(3) $14 \div 7 \times 15 - 3 =$

(4) $70 \div 10 + 9 - 3 =$

(5) $18 - 6 + 72 \div 8 =$

(6) $8 \times 4 + 30 \div 5 =$

(7) $40 - 10 + 8 =$

(8) $4 + 12 \div 6 \times 10 =$

(9) $21 - 30 \div 10 =$

(10) $9 + 4 + 3 =$

EXERCISE NO. 17

Use the right order of operations to find the answer.

(1) $7 \times 12 - 4 =$

(2) $20 - 10 + 5 =$

(3) $14 \div 7 \times 64 \div 8 =$

(4) $42 \div 7 + 16 - 4 =$

(5) $24 - 6 + 6 \times 5 =$

(6) $80 \div 10 + 9 =$

(7) $30 - 6 + 5 \times 4 =$

(8) $10 \times 9 \times 8 =$

(9) $3 + 45 \div 5 =$

(10) $6 + 48 \div 8 =$

EXERCISE NO. 18

Use the right order of operations to find the answer.

(1) $7 \times 10 + 4 =$

(2) $9 + 6 + 2 \times 9 =$

(3) $28 - 63 \div 9 =$

(4) $14 \div 7 \times 2 =$

(5) $10 + 9 \times 4 =$

(6) $8 \times 16 - 4 + 3 =$

(7) $10 - 5 \times 2 + 8 =$

(8) $9 \times 8 \times 4 \times 3 =$

(9) $3 + 5 \times 5 =$

(10) $20 \div 2 + 7 =$

EXERCISE NO. 19

Use the right order of operations to find the answer.

(1) $4 \times 40 - 8 =$

(2) $10 \div 5 \times 7 + 8 =$

(3) $4 + 4 - 2 =$

(4) $10 \times 27 \div 3 \times 5 =$

(5) $10 + 16 - 4 =$

(6) $15 - 3 \times 3 =$

(7) $8 + 36 - 9 =$

(8) $4 \times 24 - 25 - 5 =$

(9) $20 - 5 + 9 \times 7 =$

(10) $40 \div 10 + 6 =$

EXERCISE NO. 20

Use the right order of operations to find the answer.

(1) $3 \times 12 \div 4 =$

(2) $10 \div 5 + 6 + 3 =$

(3) $4 \div 2 + 9 =$

(4) $21 \div 3 + 2 =$

(5) $16 - 50 \div 5 =$

(6) $5 \times 8 \times 4 + 9 =$

(7) $7 \times 20 \div 10 \times 3 =$

(8) $16 - 4 + 24 - 8 =$

(9) $6 - 2 + 8 =$

(10) $4 \times 32 \div 8 + 2 =$

EXERCISE NO. 21

Use the right order of operations to find the answer.

(1) $10 + (4 + 63 \div 9) =$

(2) $8 \times 9 \times (4 + 5) =$

(3) $12 - 15 \div 5 =$

(4) $6 + 70 \div 14 - 7 =$

(5) $5 \times 25 - 5 =$

(6) $30 \div 10 \times 36 - 9 =$

(7) $(9 + 16 - 8) - 6 =$

(8) $(7 + 8) + 18 - 6 =$

(9) $4 + (8 + 8) - 9 =$

(10) $(2 \times 8) \times (20 - 4) =$

EXERCISE NO. 22

Use the right order of operations to find the answer.

(1) $(3 + 6) + 24 \div 6 =$

(2) $4 + 7 \times 6 =$

(3) $5 + 50 - 10 =$

(4) $(6 + 8) \times (27 \div 3) =$

(5) $9 + (10 \times 4 - 2) =$

(6) $2 + 5 \times (5 + 4) =$

(7) $(8 + 6 \times 9) - 8 =$

(8) $10 \times 18 \div 30 \div 3 =$

(9) $8 + (9 - 3) + 4 =$

(10) $(2 \times 3) + (42 \div 6) =$

EXERCISE NO. 23

Use the right order of operations to find the answer.

(1) $7 \times (4 \times 8) + 6 =$

(2) $4 + 9 + 6 =$

(3) $(48 \div 8) \times (6 \div 3) =$

(4) $(35 \div 7 + 7) + 10 =$

(5) $(21 \div 3) + 21 - 7 =$

(6) $4 \times 9 \times (9 \times 9) =$

(7) $(21 - 15 - 5) + 6 =$

(8) $8 \times (9 \times 36 \div 6) =$

(9) $35 - 20 \div 2 =$

(10) $9 \times 7 \times 7 + 7 =$

EXERCISE NO. 24

Use the right order of operations to find the answer.

(1) $5 + (30 \div 10) \times 6 =$

(2) $(5 + 12 - 6) + 3 =$

(3) $(12 - 3) - 4 \div 2 =$

(4) $(7 \times 2 \times 6) \times 9 =$

(5) $(6 \times 2) \times (20 - 10) =$

(6) $4 \times (2 + 9) \times 2 =$

(7) $(21 \div 3) \times (40 \div 5) =$

(8) $(4 + 6) - 3 \times 2 =$

(9) $4 \times 10 + (10 \times 7) =$

(10) $6 \times (7 + 5 + 4) =$

EXERCISE NO. 25

Use the right order of operations to find the answer.

(1) $9 \times 10 \times 8 + 8 =$

(2) $(16 - 4) - 24 \div 3 =$

(3) $5 \times (8 + 4 \times 6) =$

(4) $2 \times 4 + 4 =$

(5) $(7 + 4) + (2 \times 4) =$

(6) $(7 + 35 - 7) \times 6 =$

(7) $6 + 7 \times 10 =$

(8) $54 \div 9 \times (10 - 2) =$

(9) $(20 - 10 - 5) + 3 =$

(10) $4 \times (5 \times 10) - 5 =$

EXERCISE NO. 26

Use the right order of operations to find the answer.

(1) $9 + (5 + 3 \times 3) =$

(2) $(40 - 8) \times (15 \div 3) =$

(3) $(18 \div 9) + 4 - 2 =$

(4) $72 \div 9 \times (90 \div 10) =$

(5) $50 - 10 \times 2 =$

(6) $(36 \div 6) + 56 \div 8 =$

(7) $(30 - 10) \times (100 \div 10) =$

(8) $(60 \div 10 \times 9) - 5 =$

(9) $10 - 4 - 2 + 4 =$

(10) $9 \times (9 \times 3) + 2 =$

EXERCISE NO. 27

Use the right order of operations to find the answer.

(1) $(35 \div 7 \times 4) \times 6 =$

(2) $(10 - 5) + 6 + 8 =$

(3) $21 - 12 - 4 =$

(4) $5 \times (30 \div 10) - 10 =$

(5) $(8 + 6) + (5 + 5) =$

(6) $(10 + 4 \times 8) + 2 =$

(7) $4 \times 4 + (2 + 6) =$

(8) $4 \times (7 \times 4 + 4) =$

(9) $7 \times (3 \times 3) - 4 =$

(10) $10 + (9 \times 9 + 5) =$

EXERCISE NO. 28

Use the right order of operations to find the answer.

(1) $(15 \div 3) - 12 \div 6 =$

(2) $(5 + 8) \times (8 + 2) =$

(3) $8 \times (24 \div 8) - 7 =$

(4) $6 + 3 + 9 =$

(5) $5 \times (4 \times 6 - 2) =$

(6) $3 + (30 - 6 + 10) =$

(7) $9 \times 8 \times 6 =$

(8) $(8 + 10) \times (49 \div 7) =$

(9) $10 - 5 + (5 \times 7) =$

(10) $(7 + 40 - 10) \times 3 =$

EXERCISE NO. 29

Use the right order of operations to find the answer.

(1) $7 + (20 - 4 + 4) =$

(2) $6 \times 7 + 8 \times 6 =$

(3) $(6 - 3) \times (15 \div 5) =$

(4) $2 \times 2 + (6 - 2) =$

(5) $(24 - 6) \times 12 - 6 =$

(6) $(8 - 2) + 54 \div 6 =$

(7) $9 + (12 - 6) + 10 =$

(8) $5 \times (27 \div 3) - 6 =$

(9) $5 + 9 + 10 =$

(10) $27 - 9 + (8 - 2) =$

EXERCISE NO. 30

Use the right order of operations to find the answer.

(1) $(5 \times 8 \div 4) \times 10 =$

(2) $5 + (80 \div 8) \times 8 =$

(3) $(7 \times 12 \div 4) \times 6 =$

(4) $(20 - 5) \times (24 - 8) =$

(5) $(24 \div 3) + 81 \div 9 =$

(6) $5 + 15 - 5 =$

(7) $8 + 9 + (15 - 3) =$

(8) $9 + 3 \times (6 \times 2) =$

(9) $4 \times (18 - 9 + 6) =$

(10) $3 + 8 - 4 + 6 =$

EXERCISE NO. 31

Use the right order of operations to find the answer.

(1) $9 \times 9 + 8 =$

(2) $6 + 3 + (15 - 5) =$

(3) $4 + (2 \times 3 + 7) =$

(4) $15 - 20 \div 4 =$

(5) $(2 \times 8 \times 6) \times 7 =$

(6) $(12 \div 3) \times (20 \div 4) =$

(7) $(3 \times 5) + (7 \times 7) =$

(8) $9 \times 3 \times (56 \div 8) =$

(9) $9 \times 15 - 24 \div 6 =$

(10) $(12 - 4) + 4 \times 3 =$

EXERCISE NO. 32

Use the right order of operations to find the answer.

(1) $(10 + 3 + 7) - 7 =$

(2) $2 \times (3 + 9 \times 3) =$

(3) $(8 + 8) \times 4 + 6 =$

(4) $35 \div 7 \times (15 \div 3) =$

(5) $9 + 30 \div 10 =$

(6) $10 \times (10 \times 9) + 4 =$

(7) $(10 \times 7) \times (30 - 10) =$

(8) $7 \times 5 + 42 \div 6 =$

(9) $70 \div 10 + 7 \times 3 =$

(10) $3 \times (8 \times 7 + 10) =$

EXERCISE NO. 33

Use the right order of operations to find the answer.

(1) $9 + (56 \div 8 \times 10) =$

(2) $(9 - 3) \times (10 - 5) =$

(3) $(8 + 2 + 8) - 10 =$

(4) $6 + (8 + 4 \times 4) =$

(5) $10 \times (16 - 8) \times 6 =$

(6) $20 \div 4 \times 40 - 10 =$

(7) $2 \times 70 \div 7 =$

(8) $30 \div 3 \times (8 \times 9) =$

(9) $(100 \div 10) - 3 + 6 =$

(10) $9 + 3 + (5 + 3) =$

EXERCISE NO. 34

Use the right order of operations to find the answer.

(1) $(40 - 8) - 40 \div 8 =$

(2) $(12 \div 6) \times (5 \times 3) =$

(3) $(20 \div 2 \times 2) + 10 =$

(4) $8 \times 9 \times 10 =$

(5) $9 + (24 - 8) - 8 =$

(6) $3 + 7 \times 10 + 2 =$

(7) $3 + 3 + 42 \div 6 =$

(8) $8 + 9 + (6 \times 5) =$

(9) $(7 + 9) + 8 \times 6 =$

(10) $2 + (10 \times 30 - 6) =$

EXERCISE NO. 35

Use the right order of operations to find the answer.

(1) $6 + 4 + 2 =$

(2) $(2 \times 3) \times (3 + 7) =$

(3) $2 + (9 + 2 + 8) =$

(4) $2 + 5 + 18 - 9 =$

(5) $(8 + 6) + 3 \times 10 =$

(6) $5 + 5 + (15 - 3) =$

(7) $20 - 4 + (30 - 10) =$

(8) $(4 + 9) \times (2 + 10) =$

(9) $(4 \times 9 \times 7) + 6 =$

(10) $9 \times (14 - 7) - 7 =$

EXERCISE NO. 36

Use the right order of operations to find the answer.

(1) $7 + 28 \div 7 \times 8 =$

(2) $5 + 4 - 2 =$

(3) $4 \times 28 \div 4 =$

(4) $45 - 8 - 2 =$

(5) $8 \div 2 + 7 =$

(6) $40 - 10 + 40 - 10 =$

(7) $40 \div 8 - 2 =$

(8) $3 \times 12 \div 4 \times 7 =$

(9) $12 - 6 + 5 =$

(10) $28 \div 7 + 10 \div 2 =$

EXERCISE NO. 37

Use the right order of operations to find the answer.

(1) $10 \times 10 \times 5 \times 6 =$

(2) $24 - 6 + 21 \div 7 =$

(3) $3 \times 24 \div 9 - 3 =$

(4) $2 + 14 - 7 =$

(5) $7 + 10 \times 25 \div 5 =$

(6) $10 - 12 \div 4 =$

(7) $7 + 7 + 8 =$

(8) $9 \times 9 \times 7 =$

(9) $6 - 3 + 7 + 8 =$

(10) $8 \times 35 \div 5 =$

EXERCISE NO. 38

Use the right order of operations to find the answer.

(1) $8 \times 2 + 4 =$

(2) $15 \div 3 + 15 - 5 =$

(3) $3 \times 28 - 7 + 5 =$

(4) $12 - 6 + 6 =$

(5) $3 + 7 \times 10 + 6 =$

(6) $16 \div 8 + 4 =$

(7) $9 + 7 \times 6 =$

(8) $4 \times 24 \div 4 =$

(9) $40 - 42 \div 6 =$

(10) $18 - 9 + 30 - 6 =$

EXERCISE NO. 39

Use the right order of operations to find the answer.

(1) $5 + 42 \div 7 =$

(2) $8 + 4 + 8 =$

(3) $14 - 14 \div 2 =$

(4) $4 \times 2 \times 9 =$

(5) $5 \times 7 + 18 - 6 =$

(6) $35 \div 5 + 10 =$

(7) $10 + 15 \div 5 \times 5 =$

(8) $10 + 32 \div 8 + 5 =$

(9) $9 \times 8 \times 5 \times 7 =$

(10) $63 \div 9 \times 36 - 9 =$

EXERCISE NO. 40

Use the right order of operations to find the answer.

(1) $(6 \times 8) \times 2 \times 2 =$

(2) $(10 \times 9) \times 14 - 7 =$

(3) $6 + (8 \times 8) - 4 =$

(4) $5 \times (8 \times 10) - 3 =$

(5) $10 + (4 + 16 - 4) =$

(6) $(2 \times 7 \times 2) \times 3 =$

(7) $(5 + 10) + (5 + 5) =$

(8) $3 \times 8 \times 15 - 5 =$

(9) $(2 + 6) + (12 - 4) =$

(10) $8 + 3 + (12 - 4) =$

EXERCISE NO. 41

Use the right order of operations to find the answer.

(1) $35 - 7 + 10 =$

(2) $40 - 8 + 20 \div 4 =$

(3) $5 + (16 \div 8) + 5 =$

(4) $(2 + 20 - 5) - 4 =$

(5) $(6 + 9) + (20 - 5) =$

(6) $3 + (3 \times 6) + 9 =$

(7) $7 \times 70 \div 10 =$

(8) $5 \times 10 + 10 + 9 =$

(9) $4 \times (4 + 20 - 10) =$

(10) $(9 \times 3) \times (10 + 2) =$

EXERCISE NO. 42

Use the right order of operations to find the answer.

(1) $(10 \times 7 + 2) \times 2 =$

(2) $3 + 24 \div 6 =$

(3) $(10 + 8) - 12 \div 4 =$

(4) $12 - 4 + 80 \div 8 =$

(5) $(15 - 8 - 4) \times 9 =$

(6) $14 \div 2 \times 10 - 2 =$

(7) $6 + 5 \times 3 =$

(8) $(8 - 4) + (5 \times 2) =$

(9) $9 \times (6 - 3) \times 5 =$

(10) $3 + (36 - 9 \times 4) =$

EXERCISE NO. 43

Use the right order of operations to find the answer.

(1) $54 \div 6 \times (8 - 4) =$

(2) $6 + 40 - 8 =$

(3) $8 + 3 \times (6 - 2) =$

(4) $8 + (64 \div 8) - 4 =$

(5) $(6 + 35 \div 5) - 4 =$

(6) $(10 \times 6) + (8 + 9) =$

(7) $(45 - 9) \times 5 + 4 =$

(8) $7 \times (45 - 9) \times 3 =$

(9) $6 \times 5 + 72 \div 8 =$

(10) $(4 + 12 - 4) \times 10 =$

EXERCISE NO. 44

Use the right order of operations to find the answer.

(1) $16 \div 2 \times (30 \div 3) =$

(2) $7 + (24 - 6) + 5 =$

(3) $18 \div 2 + 40 - 8 =$

(4) $(24 \div 4) \times 25 - 5 =$

(5) $3 + (12 - 4 + 8) =$

(6) $(9 \times 6 + 4) \times 6 =$

(7) $10 \times (10 \times 4) - 4 =$

(8) $8 + (10 \times 2 + 9) =$

(9) $(3 \times 3) \times (5 + 5) =$

(10) $(63 \div 9) - 6 + 7 =$

EXERCISE NO. 45

Use the right order of operations to find the answer.

(1) $(42 \div 7) + (2 + 5) =$

(2) $80 \div 8 - 2 =$

(3) $20 - 4 + (15 - 3) =$

(4) $2 + (7 + 4 + 2) =$

(5) $2 + 10 - 5 =$

(6) $(9 + 4) - 10 \div 5 =$

(7) $2 \times (8 - 4) - 4 =$

(8) $(7 \times 12 - 6) \times 3 =$

(9) $6 - 2 \times 2 + 4 =$

(10) $9 + (7 + 4 + 6) =$

ANSWERS!

EXERCISE NO. 1

(1) $6 \times 27 \div 9 = 18$

(2) $5 \times 10 \times 4 = 200$

(3) $4 + 6 + 6 = 16$

(4) $42 \div 7 \times 7 = 42$

(5) $9 \times 9 \times 3 = 243$

(6) $9 + 8 + 35 - 7 = 45$

(7) $12 - 6 + 12 - 6 = 12$

(8) $4 + 3 + 6 + 5 = 18$

(9) $15 - 3 + 10 + 7 = 29$

(10) $9 \times 32 \div 8 = 36$

EXERCISE NO. 2

(1) $40 \div 10 \times 2 = 8$

(2) $15 \div 5 + 3 = 6$

(3) $8 + 6 \times 21 - 7 = 127$

(4) $5 \times 7 + 4 = 39$

(5) $9 \times 10 + 6 = 96$

(6) $3 + 4 + 4 = 11$

(7) $10 - 5 + 70 \div 10 = 12$

(8) $10 \times 5 + 7 = 57$

(9) $6 \times 4 \times 6 = 144$

(10) $3 \times 8 \div 4 + 7 = 13$

EXERCISE NO. 3

(1) $36 \div 6 \times 3 = 18$

(2) $7 + 9 \times 2 = 25$

(3) $6 \times 10 + 56 \div 7 = 68$

(4) $6 + 15 \div 5 = 9$

(5) $4 \times 8 \times 8 \div 4 = 64$

(6) $6 + 6 + 7 \times 9 = 75$

(7) $80 \div 10 \times 7 = 56$

(8) $25 - 5 + 42 \div 6 = 27$

(9) $3 + 50 \div 5 = 13$

(10) $9 + 2 + 3 = 14$

EXERCISE NO. 4

(1) $2 + 6 + 2 \times 9 = 26$

(2) $10 \div 5 + 8 = 10$

(3) $5 \times 2 + 3 = 13$

(4) $8 \times 10 + 18 - 9 = 89$

(5) $3 \times 54 \div 9 = 18$

(6) $8 \times 5 + 5 = 45$

(7) $8 - 2 + 3 = 9$

(8) $6 \times 5 + 6 = 36$

(9) $2 \times 16 - 4 = 28$

(10) $7 + 6 \times 9 \times 6 = 331$

EXERCISE NO. 5

(1) $5 \times 25 - 5 = 120$

(2) $48 \div 8 + 7 = 13$

(3) $5 \times 42 \div 7 = 30$

(4) $4 + 70 \div 10 \times 2 = 18$

(5) $5 \times 14 - 48 \div 8 = 64$

(6) $6 + 5 + 48 \div 6 = 19$

(7) $20 \div 2 + 2 = 12$

(8) $8 + 16 - 4 = 20$

(9) $3 + 9 + 4 = 16$

(10) $5 \times 30 - 10 \times 9 = 60$

EXERCISE NO. 6

(1) $6 + 10 + 50 \div 10 = 21$

(2) $4 + 12 - 4 = 12$

(3) $2 + 8 + 32 \div 8 = 14$

(4) $9 - 14 \div 2 = 2$

(5) $2 \times 27 - 9 = 45$

(6) $10 \times 6 - 2 = 58$

(7) $24 \div 8 + 8 = 11$

(8) $3 \times 35 - 32 - 8 = 65$

(9) $20 - 9 - 3 = 8$

(10) $8 \times 20 - 5 \times 3 = 145$

EXERCISE NO. 7

(1) $10 \times 20 - 4 = 196$

(2) $40 - 8 + 7 + 9 = 48$

(3) $6 + 3 + 8 + 10 = 27$

(4) $2 + 5 \times 8 \times 6 = 242$

(5) $5 + 10 - 2 = 13$

(6) $8 - 4 + 2 \times 7 = 18$

(7) $2 + 54 \div 6 = 11$

(8) $2 \times 8 \times 8 = 128$

(9) $2 \times 12 \div 4 = 6$

(10) $9 \times 12 \div 2 + 6 = 60$

EXERCISE NO. 8

(1) $40 - 15 - 5 = 20$

(2) $3 \times 64 \div 8 = 24$

(3) $6 \times 9 \div 3 + 7 = 25$

(4) $2 + 8 \times 4 \times 7 = 226$

(5) $5 + 8 + 6 \times 10 = 73$

(6) $5 + 10 \times 8 + 2 = 87$

(7) $10 \times 7 + 2 = 72$

(8) $7 \times 12 - 6 = 78$

(9) $9 + 9 - 3 = 15$

(10) $8 + 3 \times 3 = 17$

EXERCISE NO. 9

(1) $2 + 5 \times 9 = 47$

(2) $8 \times 8 + 4 \times 10 = 104$

(3) $12 - 4 + 2 = 10$

(4) $25 \div 5 + 3 = 8$

(5) $8 + 4 + 24 - 8 = 28$

(6) $70 \div 7 \times 7 = 70$

(7) $8 - 2 + 2 + 2 = 10$

(8) $5 \times 14 - 7 = 63$

(9) $3 + 12 - 6 = 9$

(10) $7 + 8 + 20 - 5 = 30$

EXERCISE NO. 10

(1) $10 - 2 + 2 = 10$

(2) $7 \times 10 - 2 = 68$

(3) $72 \div 9 + 16 \div 2 = 16$

(4) $14 \div 7 \times 12 \div 3 = 8$

(5) $8 + 6 + 28 \div 7 = 18$

(6) $4 \times 20 - 8 - 2 = 70$

(7) $21 \div 7 \times 6 = 18$

(8) $15 \div 5 \times 6 \times 3 = 54$

(9) $24 \div 3 + 5 = 13$

(10) $5 + 6 \times 3 = 23$

EXERCISE NO. 11

(1) $32 \div 8 \times 9 + 8 = 44$

(2) $7 + 10 + 7 = 24$

(3) $2 + 35 \div 5 + 6 = 15$

(4) $8 + 30 - 27 \div 9 = 35$

(5) $50 - 10 \div 2 = 45$

(6) $30 - 10 + 3 = 23$

(7) $4 - 2 + 6 = 8$

(8) $10 \times 2 \times 7 = 140$

(9) $6 + 40 \div 10 = 10$

(10) $9 \times 24 \div 8 + 9 = 36$

EXERCISE NO. 12

(1) $36 \div 12 \div 3 + 3 = 4$

(2) $3 + 35 - 7 = 31$

(3) $27 \div 3 + 6 \times 5 = 39$

(4) $2 + 5 \times 4 + 5 = 27$

(5) $9 \times 40 \div 5 = 72$

(6) $8 \times 3 + 7 = 31$

(7) $9 \times 49 \div 7 = 63$

(8) $3 \times 28 - 21 \div 7 = 81$

(9) $8 + 28 - 16 - 8 = 12$

(10) $20 \div 2 + 8 = 18$

EXERCISE NO. 13

(1) $16 \div 8 + 30 - 6 = 26$

(2) $4 + 3 + 9 = 16$

(3) $14 \div 2 + 6 = 13$

(4) $8 \times 14 - 7 = 105$

(5) $9 + 6 + 6 - 2 = 19$

(6) $6 + 24 \div 8 - 4 = 5$

(7) $7 + 7 + 7 = 21$

(8) $30 \div 6 + 24 \div 4 = 11$

(9) $21 - 6 - 2 \times 4 = 7$

(10) $18 \div 9 \times 7 = 14$

EXERCISE NO. 14

(1) $18 \div 2 + 8 + 8 = 25$

(2) $8 \times 6 + 4 = 52$

(3) $7 + 25 - 5 = 27$

(4) $36 - 48 \div 12 \div 2 = 34$

(5) $10 \times 10 \div 2 + 8 = 58$

(6) $4 \times 3 + 8 = 20$

(7) $32 - 15 \div 5 + 7 = 36$

(8) $30 \div 5 + 8 + 10 = 24$

(9) $5 \times 10 \times 10 = 500$

(10) $9 \times 3 \times 6 = 162$

(1) $9 + 2 + 9 = 20$

(2) $7 + 20 - 4 = 23$

(3) $10 \times 3 + 18 - 9 = 39$

(4) $32 - 9 - 3 = 20$

(5) $63 \div 7 \times 6 \div 2 = 27$

(6) $8 \times 3 + 3 = 27$

(7) $15 - 5 + 2 + 8 = 20$

(8) $60 \div 4 - 2 = 13$

(9) $18 - 10 - 2 = 6$

(10) $4 \times 4 + 2 = 18$

(1) $30 - 6 \times 3 + 4 = 16$

(2) $6 \times 90 \div 9 = 60$

(3) $14 \div 7 \times 15 - 3 = 27$

(4) $70 \div 10 + 9 - 3 = 13$

(5) $18 - 6 + 72 \div 8 = 21$

(6) $8 \times 4 + 30 \div 5 = 38$

(7) $40 - 10 + 8 = 38$

(8) $4 + 12 \div 6 \times 10 = 24$

(9) $21 - 30 \div 10 = 18$

(10) $9 + 4 + 3 = 16$

(1) $7 \times 12 - 4 = 80$

(2) $20 - 10 + 5 = 15$

(3) $14 \div 7 \times 64 \div 8 = 16$

(4) $42 \div 7 + 16 - 4 = 18$

(5) $24 - 6 + 6 \times 5 = 48$

(6) $80 \div 10 + 9 = 17$

(7) $30 - 6 + 5 \times 4 = 44$

(8) $10 \times 9 \times 8 = 720$

(9) $3 + 45 \div 5 = 12$

(10) $6 + 48 \div 8 = 12$

(1) $7 \times 10 + 4 = 74$

(2) $9 + 6 + 2 \times 9 = 33$

(3) $28 - 63 \div 9 = 21$

(4) $14 \div 7 \times 2 = 4$

(5) $10 + 9 \times 4 = 46$

(6) $8 \times 16 - 4 + 3 = 127$

(7) $10 - 5 \times 2 + 8 = 8$

(8) $9 \times 8 \times 4 \times 3 = 864$

(9) $3 + 5 \times 5 = 28$

(10) $20 \div 2 + 7 = 17$

EXERCISE NO. 19

(1) $4 \times 40 - 8 = 152$

(2) $10 \div 5 \times 7 + 8 = 22$

(3) $4 + 4 - 2 = 6$

(4) $10 \times 27 \div 3 \times 5 = 450$

(5) $10 + 16 - 4 = 22$

(6) $15 - 3 \times 3 = 6$

(7) $8 + 36 - 9 = 35$

(8) $4 \times 24 - 25 - 5 = 66$

(9) $20 - 5 + 9 \times 7 = 78$

(10) $40 \div 10 + 6 = 10$

EXERCISE NO. 20

(1) $3 \times 12 \div 4 = 9$

(2) $10 \div 5 + 6 + 3 = 11$

(3) $4 \div 2 + 9 = 11$

(4) $21 \div 3 + 2 = 9$

(5) $16 - 50 \div 5 = 6$

(6) $5 \times 8 \times 4 + 9 = 169$

(7) $7 \times 20 \div 10 \times 3 = 42$

(8) $16 - 4 + 24 - 8 = 28$

(9) $6 - 2 + 8 = 12$

(10) $4 \times 32 \div 8 + 2 = 18$

EXERCISE NO. 21

(1) $10 + (4 + 63 \div 9) = 21$

(2) $8 \times 9 \times (4 + 5) = 648$

(3) $12 - 15 \div 5 = 9$

(4) $6 + 70 \div 14 - 7 = 4$

(5) $5 \times 25 - 5 = 120$

(6) $30 \div 10 \times 36 - 9 = 99$

(7) $(9 + 16 - 8) - 6 = 11$

(8) $(7 + 8) + 18 - 6 = 27$

(9) $4 + (8 + 8) - 9 = 11$

(10) $(2 \times 8) \times (20 - 4) = 256$

EXERCISE NO. 22

(1) $(3 + 6) + 24 \div 6 = 13$

(2) $4 + 7 \times 6 = 46$

(3) $5 + 50 - 10 = 45$

(4) $(6 + 8) \times (27 \div 3) = 126$

(5) $9 + (10 \times 4 - 2) = 47$

(6) $2 + 5 \times (5 + 4) = 47$

(7) $(8 + 6 \times 9) - 8 = 54$

(8) $10 \times 18 \div 30 \div 3 = 2$

(9) $8 + (9 - 3) + 4 = 18$

(10) $(2 \times 3) + (42 \div 6) = 13$

(1) $7 \times (4 \times 8) + 6 = 230$

(2) $4 + 9 + 6 = 19$

(3) $(48 \div 8) \times (6 \div 3) = 12$

(4) $(35 \div 7 + 7) + 10 = 22$

(5) $(21 \div 3) + 21 - 7 = 21$

(6) $4 \times 9 \times (9 \times 9) = 2916$

(7) $(21 - 15 - 5) + 6 = 7$

(8) $8 \times (9 \times 36 \div 6) = 432$

(9) $35 - 20 \div 2 = 25$

(10) $9 \times 7 \times 7 + 7 = 448$

EXERCISE NO. 24

(1) $5 + (30 \div 10) \times 6 = 23$

(2) $(5 + 12 - 6) + 3 = 14$

(3) $(12 - 3) - 4 \div 2 = 7$

(4) $(7 \times 2 \times 6) \times 9 = 756$

(5) $(6 \times 2) \times (20 - 10) = 120$

(6) $4 \times (2 + 9) \times 2 = 88$

(7) $(21 \div 3) \times (40 \div 5) = 56$

(8) $(4 + 6) - 3 \times 2 = 4$

(9) $4 \times 10 + (10 \times 7) = 110$

(10) $6 \times (7 + 5 + 4) = 96$

EXERCISE NO. 25

(1) $9 \times 10 \times 8 + 8 = 728$

(2) $(16 - 4) - 24 \div 3 = 4$

(3) $5 \times (8 + 4 \times 6) = 160$

(4) $2 \times 4 + 4 = 12$

(5) $(7 + 4) + (2 \times 4) = 19$

(6) $(7 + 35 - 7) \times 6 = 210$

(7) $6 + 7 \times 10 = 76$

(8) $54 \div 9 \times (10 - 2) = 48$

(9) $(20 - 10 - 5) + 3 = 8$

(10) $4 \times (5 \times 10) - 5 = 195$

EXERCISE NO. 26

(1) $9 + (5 + 3 \times 3) = 23$

(2) $(40 - 8) \times (15 \div 3) = 160$

(3) $(18 \div 9) + 4 - 2 = 4$

(4) $72 \div 9 \times (90 \div 10) = 72$

(5) $50 - 10 \times 2 = 30$

(6) $(36 \div 6) + 56 \div 8 = 13$

(7) $(30 - 10) \times (100 \div 10) = 200$

(8) $(60 \div 10 \times 9) - 5 = 49$

(9) $10 - 4 - 2 + 4 = 8$

(10) $9 \times (9 \times 3) + 2 = 245$

EXERCISE NO. 27

(1) $(35 \div 7 \times 4) \times 6 = 120$

(2) $(10 - 5) + 6 + 8 = 19$

(3) $21 - 12 - 4 = 5$

(4) $5 \times (30 \div 10) - 10 = 5$

(5) $(8 + 6) + (5 + 5) = 24$

(6) $(10 + 4 \times 8) + 2 = 44$

(7) $4 \times 4 + (2 + 6) = 24$

(8) $4 \times (7 \times 4 + 4) = 128$

(9) $7 \times (3 \times 3) - 4 = 59$

(10) $10 + (9 \times 9 + 5) = 96$

EXERCISE NO. 28

(1) $(15 \div 3) - 12 \div 6 = 3$

(2) $(5 + 8) \times (8 + 2) = 130$

(3) $8 \times (24 \div 8) - 7 = 17$

(4) $6 + 3 + 9 = 18$

(5) $5 \times (4 \times 6 - 2) = 110$

(6) $3 + (30 - 6 + 10) = 37$

(7) $9 \times 8 \times 6 = 432$

(8) $(8 + 10) \times (49 \div 7) = 126$

(9) $10 - 5 + (5 \times 7) = 40$

(10) $(7 + 40 - 10) \times 3 = 111$

EXERCISE NO. 29

(1) $7 + (20 - 4 + 4) = 27$

(2) $6 \times 7 + 8 \times 6 = 90$

(3) $(6 - 3) \times (15 \div 5) = 9$

(4) $2 \times 2 + (6 - 2) = 8$

(5) $(24 - 6) \times 12 - 6 = 210$

(6) $(8 - 2) + 54 \div 6 = 15$

(7) $9 + (12 - 6) + 10 = 25$

(8) $5 \times (27 \div 3) - 6 = 39$

(9) $5 + 9 + 10 = 24$

(10) $27 - 9 + (8 - 2) = 24$

EXERCISE NO. 30

(1) $(5 \times 8 \div 4) \times 10 = 100$

(2) $5 + (80 \div 8) \times 8 = 85$

(3) $(7 \times 12 \div 4) \times 6 = 126$

(4) $(20 - 5) \times (24 - 8) = 240$

(5) $(24 \div 3) + 81 \div 9 = 17$

(6) $5 + 15 - 5 = 15$

(7) $8 + 9 + (15 - 3) = 29$

(8) $9 + 3 \times (6 \times 2) = 45$

(9) $4 \times (18 - 9 + 6) = 60$

(10) $3 + 8 - 4 + 6 = 13$

(1) $9 \times 9 + 8 = 89$

(2) $6 + 3 + (15 - 5) = 19$

(3) $4 + (2 \times 3 + 7) = 17$

(4) $15 - 20 \div 4 = 10$

(5) $(2 \times 8 \times 6) \times 7 = 672$

(6) $(12 \div 3) \times (20 \div 4) = 20$

(7) $(3 \times 5) + (7 \times 7) = 64$

(8) $9 \times 3 \times (56 \div 8) = 189$

(9) $9 \times 15 - 24 \div 6 = 131$

(10) $(12 - 4) + 4 \times 3 = 20$

(1) $(10 + 3 + 7) - 7 = 13$

(2) $2 \times (3 + 9 \times 3) = 60$

(3) $(8 + 8) \times 4 + 6 = 70$

(4) $35 \div 7 \times (15 \div 3) = 25$

(5) $9 + 30 \div 10 = 12$

(6) $10 \times (10 \times 9) + 4 = 904$

(7) $(10 \times 7) \times (30 - 10) = 1400$

(8) $7 \times 5 + 42 \div 6 = 42$

(9) $70 \div 10 + 7 \times 3 = 28$

(10) $3 \times (8 \times 7 + 10) = 198$

(1) $9 + (56 \div 8 \times 10) = 79$

(2) $(9 - 3) \times (10 - 5) = 30$

(3) $(8 + 2 + 8) - 10 = 8$

(4) $6 + (8 + 4 \times 4) = 30$

(5) $10 \times (16 - 8) \times 6 = 480$

(6) $20 \div 4 \times 40 - 10 = 190$

(7) $2 \times 70 \div 7 = 20$

(8) $30 \div 3 \times (8 \times 9) = 720$

(9) $(100 \div 10) - 3 + 6 = 13$

(10) $9 + 3 + (5 + 3) = 20$

(1) $(40 - 8) - 40 \div 8 = 27$

(2) $(12 \div 6) \times (5 \times 3) = 30$

(3) $(20 \div 2 \times 2) + 10 = 30$

(4) $8 \times 9 \times 10 = 720$

(5) $9 + (24 - 8) - 8 = 17$

(6) $3 + 7 \times 10 + 2 = 75$

(7) $3 + 3 + 42 \div 6 = 13$

(8) $8 + 9 + (6 \times 5) = 47$

(9) $(7 + 9) + 8 \times 6 = 64$

(10) $2 + (10 \times 30 - 6) = 296$

EXERCISE NO. 35

(1) $6 + 4 + 2 = 12$

(2) $(2 \times 3) \times (3 + 7) = 60$

(3) $2 + (9 + 2 + 8) = 21$

(4) $2 + 5 + 18 - 9 = 16$

(5) $(8 + 6) + 3 \times 10 = 44$

(6) $5 + 5 + (15 - 3) = 22$

(7) $20 - 4 + (30 - 10) = 36$

(8) $(4 + 9) \times (2 + 10) = 156$

(9) $(4 \times 9 \times 7) + 6 = 258$

(10) $9 \times (14 - 7) - 7 = 56$

EXERCISE NO. 36

(1) $7 + 28 \div 7 \times 8 = 39$

(2) $5 + 4 - 2 = 7$

(3) $4 \times 28 \div 4 = 28$

(4) $45 - 8 - 2 = 35$

(5) $8 \div 2 + 7 = 11$

(6) $40 - 10 + 40 - 10 = 60$

(7) $40 \div 8 - 2 = 3$

(8) $3 \times 12 \div 4 \times 7 = 63$

(9) $12 - 6 + 5 = 11$

(10) $28 \div 7 + 10 \div 2 = 9$

EXERCISE NO. 37

(1) $10 \times 10 \times 5 \times 6 = 3000$

(2) $24 - 6 + 21 \div 7 = 21$

(3) $3 \times 24 \div 9 - 3 = 5$

(4) $2 + 14 - 7 = 9$

(5) $7 + 10 \times 25 \div 5 = 57$

(6) $10 - 12 \div 4 = 7$

(7) $7 + 7 + 8 = 22$

(8) $9 \times 9 \times 7 = 567$

(9) $6 - 3 + 7 + 8 = 18$

(10) $8 \times 35 \div 5 = 56$

EXERCISE NO. 38

(1) $8 \times 2 + 4 = 20$

(2) $15 \div 3 + 15 - 5 = 15$

(3) $3 \times 28 - 7 + 5 = 82$

(4) $12 - 6 + 6 = 12$

(5) $3 + 7 \times 10 + 6 = 79$

(6) $16 \div 8 + 4 = 6$

(7) $9 + 7 \times 6 = 51$

(8) $4 \times 24 \div 4 = 24$

(9) $40 - 42 \div 6 = 33$

(10) $18 - 9 + 30 - 6 = 33$

EXERCISE NO. 39

(1) $5 + 42 \div 7 = 11$

(2) $8 + 4 + 8 = 20$

(3) $14 - 14 \div 2 = 7$

(4) $4 \times 2 \times 9 = 72$

(5) $5 \times 7 + 18 - 6 = 47$

(6) $35 \div 5 + 10 = 17$

(7) $10 + 15 \div 5 \times 5 = 25$

(8) $10 + 32 \div 8 + 5 = 19$

(9) $9 \times 8 \times 5 \times 7 = 2520$

(10) $63 \div 9 \times 36 - 9 = 243$

EXERCISE NO. 40

(1) $(6 \times 8) \times 2 \times 2 = 192$

(2) $(10 \times 9) \times 14 - 7 = 1253$

(3) $6 + (8 \times 8) - 4 = 66$

(4) $5 \times (8 \times 10) - 3 = 397$

(5) $10 + (4 + 16 - 4) = 26$

(6) $(2 \times 7 \times 2) \times 3 = 84$

(7) $(5 + 10) + (5 + 5) = 25$

(8) $3 \times 8 \times 15 - 5 = 355$

(9) $(2 + 6) + (12 - 4) = 16$

(10) $8 + 3 + (12 - 4) = 19$

EXERCISE NO. 41

(1) $35 - 7 + 10 = 38$

(2) $40 - 8 + 20 \div 4 = 37$

(3) $5 + (16 \div 8) + 5 = 12$

(4) $(2 + 20 - 5) - 4 = 13$

(5) $(6 + 9) + (20 - 5) = 30$

(6) $3 + (3 \times 6) + 9 = 30$

(7) $7 \times 70 \div 10 = 49$

(8) $5 \times 10 + 10 + 9 = 69$

(9) $4 \times (4 + 20 - 10) = 56$

(10) $(9 \times 3) \times (10 + 2) = 324$

EXERCISE NO. 42

(1) $(10 \times 7 + 2) \times 2 = 144$

(2) $3 + 24 \div 6 = 7$

(3) $(10 + 8) - 12 \div 4 = 15$

(4) $12 - 4 + 80 \div 8 = 18$

(5) $(15 - 8 - 4) \times 9 = 27$

(6) $14 \div 2 \times 10 - 2 = 68$

(7) $6 + 5 \times 3 = 21$

(8) $(8 - 4) + (5 \times 2) = 14$

(9) $9 \times (6 - 3) \times 5 = 135$

(10) $3 + (36 - 9 \times 4) = 3$

EXERCISE NO. 43

(1) $54 \div 6 \times (8 - 4) = 36$

(2) $6 + 40 - 8 = 38$

(3) $8 + 3 \times (6 - 2) = 20$

(4) $8 + (64 \div 8) - 4 = 12$

(5) $(6 + 35 \div 5) - 4 = 9$

(6) $(10 \times 6) + (8 + 9) = 77$

(7) $(45 - 9) \times 5 + 4 = 184$

(8) $7 \times (45 - 9) \times 3 = 756$

(9) $6 \times 5 + 72 \div 8 = 39$

(10) $(4 + 12 - 4) \times 10 = 120$

EXERCISE NO. 44

(1) $16 \div 2 \times (30 \div 3) = 80$

(2) $7 + (24 - 6) + 5 = 30$

(3) $18 \div 2 + 40 - 8 = 41$

(4) $(24 \div 4) \times 25 - 5 = 145$

(5) $3 + (12 - 4 + 8) = 19$

(6) $(9 \times 6 + 4) \times 6 = 348$

(7) $10 \times (10 \times 4) - 4 = 396$

(8) $8 + (10 \times 2 + 9) = 37$

(9) $(3 \times 3) \times (5 + 5) = 90$

(10) $(63 \div 9) - 6 + 7 = 8$

EXERCISE NO. 45

(1) $(42 \div 7) + (2 + 5) = 13$

(2) $80 \div 8 - 2 = 8$

(3) $20 - 4 + (15 - 3) = 28$

(4) $2 + (7 + 4 + 2) = 15$

(5) $2 + 10 - 5 = 7$

(6) $(9 + 4) - 10 \div 5 = 11$

(7) $2 \times (8 - 4) - 4 = 4$

(8) $(7 \times 12 - 6) \times 3 = 234$

(9) $6 - 2 \times 2 + 4 = 6$

(10) $9 + (7 + 4 + 6) = 26$

Visit
BABY PROFESSOR
EDUCATION KIDS
www.BabyProfessorBooks.com
to download Free Baby Professor eBooks and view
our catalog of new and exciting Children's Books